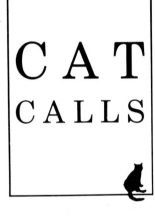

CAT
CALLS

CAT
CALLS

CAT-EGORIES FOR
THE NAMING
OF CATS

WEIDENFELD & NICOLSON
LONDON

CREATED AND PRODUCED BY PHOEBE PHILLIPS EDITIONS
DESIGN: IVOR CLAYDON

ILLUSTRATIONS: KAREN DAWS
TEXT: ALASTAIR MACGREGOR

PRINTED AND BOUND IN ITALY

ISBN: 0 297 79440 X

They say that the test (of literary power) is whether a man can write an inscription. I say, can he name a kitten. And by this test, I am condemned, for I cannot.

SAMUEL BUTLER (1835–1902)

CONTENTS

INTRODUCTION
PAGE 8

LITERARY CATS
PAGE 10

FAMOUS CATS AND FAMOUS PEOPLE'S CATS
PAGE 20

LEGENDARY CATS
PAGE 30

RECORD-BREAKING CATS
PAGE 34

BLACK CATS
PAGE 38

ABYSSINIAN CATS
PAGE 65

WHITE CATS
PAGE 44

SIAMESE CATS
PAGE 67

GINGER CATS
PAGE 50

BURMESE CATS
PAGE 70

GREY CATS
PAGE 53

MANX CATS
PAGE 73

CALICO CATS
PAGE 55

RUSSIAN BLUES
PAGE 76

TABBY CATS
PAGE 58

JUST CATS
PAGE 79

LONG-HAIRED CATS
PAGE 61

INDEX
PAGE 87

INTRODUCTION

In *Old Possum's Book of Practical Cats*, T. S. Eliot asserts that every cat should have three names: one each for its owner and feline friends, and one known only to itself.

For the human being in a cat's life, finding even the one name that matches the uniqueness of its individual personality is a serious and challenging task. To call a creature of plebeian disposition and preference Sir Piers Courcy de Courcy will only confuse it and provoke other cats – and the neighbours – into unseemly mirth.

More proletarian names, on the other hand, don't do justice to an animal whose ancestors were worshipped in ancient Egypt – to the point that anyone who mistreated them was put to death – venerated in classical Greece and Rome – where soothsayers regarded them with the greatest respect – and abominably treated in medieval and later times: although there were private pets, cats were regarded as witches' familiars and acolytes of the Devil, fit only to be thrown into fires, hurled in batches off high towers, skinned alive . . . .

In England, they were more sympathetically regarded by the eighteenth century: Dr Samuel Johnson and Isaac Newton both doted on their pets. But nineteenth-century France was one of the first places where the clock was turned back to the days when cats were widely respected and loved. Many French writers and painters, especially, admired them to the point of obsession. In the United States, which today has the world's highest cat ownership, famous cat owners included Abraham Lincoln and Mark Twain.

Cat Calls lists more than 300 names, starting with some of the cats and kittens immortalized by European, English and American writers, for owners with literary ambitions. The names of famous cats – and of cats belonging to famous people – come next, followed by those of legendary and then record-breaking felines. All these are suitable for a cat of any – or no – breed or pedigree, provided its character and personality match the name.

The chapters that follow deal with specific categories from black, white, grey and ginger to Siamese and Burmese, Abyssinian cats and Russian blues.

Finally, there are names for animals that are Just Cats – all those mysterious feline friends, provokers and comforters, who fall into no particular category, but who often combine the best features of a variety of breeds.

To them, and all cats and their owners, this book of 'cat calls' is dedicated.

LITERARY CATS

The book spines read:
POSSUMS BOOK OF PRACTICAL CATS — T.S. ELLIOT
WHAT KITTY DID NEXT! — T. KITTEN
CAT ON A HOT TIN ROOF — BLACKIE
THREE LITTLE KITTENS — OBAM PRESS.
A TAIL OF TWO CITIES — WILLUM.
THE OWL AND THE PUSSYCAT — E. LEAR.
THE MEWS — T. TAILS
— TABBY PRESS.
TOM CAT — C. LITTER

ARISTO-CATS　　The Walt Disney characters, and group of that name; somewhere there must be a jazz combo – or even a chamber-music quartet.

ASPARAGUS　　The 'real' name of T.S. Eliot's Gus the Theatre Cat, once a famous star who acted on the English stage with Sir Henry Irving. Eliot wrote a set of poems published as *Old Possum's Book of Practical Cats* and the wonderful and individually named cats, originally illustrated by Nicolas Bentley, were transmuted into theatrical history when the only musical to feature an entire cast of cats became a long-running hit in England and the United States. With music by Andrew Lloyd Webber, and at least one best-selling song, 'Memories', *Cats* is now a legend.

BELLCAT　　From Aesop's *Fables* – the bell around his neck meant that his prey had good warning.

BUSTOPHER JONES　　The Cat About Town of T.S. Eliot's characters; hospitable, suave and elegant, but grown fat from the good life.

CAT

Holly Golightly's cat in *Breakfast at Tiffany's*, a story by Truman Capote which became a film with an even more popular theme song, 'Moon River'.

CHESHIRE CAT

Lewis Carroll's shadowy cat from *Alice in Wonderland*, who disappears at will, leaving nothing behind but his smile.

DINAH

Belonged to Alice in her 'real' life before she fell down the hole.

FELISSA

The feline heroine of an anonymous tale with a moral, published in 1811.

FELIX

The most famous of cartoon cats, drawn by Pat Sullivan; he first delighted children at Saturday morning film shows in the 1920s.

FRANCOIS

A cat with a cruel hard gaze, a diabolic stare, from *Thérèse Raquin*, Emile Zola's tale of passion and remorse.

GALLOP	The hero of English poet Stevie Smith's 'Galloping Cat'.
GIB	*How Gib Disturbed the Wedding Feast* by Ravenscroft, *c.* 1611; the story of the wedding of a frog and a mouse, scene of joyous celebration until Gib the Cat came in and ate the mouse bride.
GROWLTIGER	Another cat from *Old Possum*: a rough barge cat known as 'The Terror of the Thames' who hated foreign cats because his ear had been torn by a Siamese, and came to a terrible end, forced to walk the plank.
HIDDIGEIGEI	The tom cat hero of 'Der Trompeter von Sakkinger', a long poem by the German poet Joseph Victor von Scheffel. A restaurant in Capri was named after him.
HURLYBURLY-BUSS RUMPEL-STIZCHEN	Putative feline authors of lines to Poet Laureate Robert Southey. Carl van Vechten, author of *The Tiger in the House*, described the verses as sentimental and silly: 'No cat, it would seem, could write so ill.'

JACOBINA	A brindled cat in Bulwer-Lytton's *Eugene Aram*. 'Daughter, wife and friend' of Corporal Bunting, whom she loved with unique devotion, she learnt to 'fly as if she were mad at anyone upon whom the corporal saw fit to set her'.
JENNIE	The eponymous tabby stray of Paul Gallico's novel.
JENNYANYDOTS	An Eliot cat who sits and sits and sits and sits...

LADY JANE	A ferocious beast in *Bleak House*, by Charles Dickens.
KALLICRATES	An orange Persian cat in *Blind Alley* by W.L. George, who plays the role of philosopher, critic and superior of man.
MACAVITY	Eliot's Mystery Cat from *Old Possum's Book of Practical Cats*: ginger and tall and thin, a master criminal who is never there, the Napoleon of Crime.
MALKIN	Obvious derivation from Grimalkin, first used in a curiously composed and erotic poem of the 14th century found in an English abbey.
MEHITABEL	Don Marquis' heroine of *archy and mehitabel*, a collection of poems about a cat and a cockroach; mehitabel is the wild and independent cat who doesn't want to stay at home: 'toujours gai, archy, toujours gai!' (no capitals because the cockroach couldn't hold down the shift key on the typewriter).
MINNALOUSHE	A black cat who danced under the moon, in a poem by William Butler Yeats.

MISS TABBY

A beautiful tabby-cat, so beloved by a young man that she was turned into a lovely woman: 'her solemn purring dwindled to a sigh, her tail to make a muff for her hands'. But oh! on her bridal night Miss Tabby forgot her new body and, upon seeing a mouse, sprang from the sheets, seized the trembling prey and at that moment was turned back into a cat.

MR MISTOFFELEES

The *Old Possum* Conjuring Cat, full of inventions and surprising illusions.

MUNGOJERRIE AND RUMPELTEAZER

A pair of clowning cats in Eliot's poems, who ransacked houses and stole meat from the ovens in anyone's kitchen.

OLD DEUTERONOMY
The Oldest Cat in *Cats*, famous in proverb and famous in rhyme; now even more famous with his very own *Cats* song.

ORLANDO
The Marmalade Cat, in a wonderful series written by Katherine Hale with illustrations of Orlando adventuring around the world.

PERCY
A two-timing tom in Don Marquis' *archy and mehitabel* who falsely offered mehitabel 'companionate marriage'.

PERDITA
Her name means lost. Perdita was adopted for a human heroine in *The Winter's Tale* but is also a cat celebrated by Caroline Marriage in her poem 'Nine Lives'.

PLUTO
A magnificent black cat in Edgar Allan Poe's story.

PUSS IN BOOTS
Le Chat Botte, hero of Perrault's fairy tale; the original illustrations were by Grandville.

PYEWACKET
The Siamese cat in *Bell, Book and Candle*, a play by John van Druten about delightfully wacky modern witches.

RAMINAGROBIS

From La Fontaine's *Fables*, a wise and saintly cat of the forest who solved problems by eating the animals who complained.

SELIMA

The poet Thomas Gray's pensive and elegant tabby, who drowned in a goldfish bowl.

SIMKINS

Beatrix Potter's pussycat, always busy with the housekeeping and keeping everything tidy.

SKIMBLE-SHANKS

Eliot's Railway Cat in *Old Possum's Book of Practical Cats*, who refuses to allow anything at all to go wrong on his train.

SUSIE WONG

Half-Burmese Susie Wong, heroine of the play by Paul Osborn, has given her name to many mixed-blood oriental cats.

SYLVESTER

Famous cartoon cat, partnered with Tweetie-Pie, a canary with a lisp (of 'I taut I taw a puddytat' fame) who usually wins their fights.

TOBERMORY The hero of the story by Saki (H.H. Munro). He can talk, and causes havoc with his slightly malicious gossip.

TOM Fighting cat of Tom and Jerry (the mouse) fame. The cartoons started in the 1930s following on the great success of Felix.

TURIRI A mournful beast in Pierre Loti's *Le Mariage de Loti*, who was sick almost constantly and dined off blue butterflies.

FAMOUS CATS AND FAMOUS PEOPLE'S CATS

BELAUD

A grey cat, so beautiful to her owner, Joachim du Bellay, 16th-century French poet, that he thought she should be immortal.

BEELZEBUB,
BLATHERSKIT,
BUFFALO BILL

Mark Twain's cats, who always went everywhere together.

BEPPO

A nickname for Giuseppe; Lord Byron called his cat Beppo, probably after the Venetian pirate hero of one of his poems.

BISMARCK,
DISRAELI,
GLADSTONE

Three of the 60 large Persian cats owned by Florence Nightingale.

BOMBER

After a London cat who, during World War II, used to crouch under a cooker when German bombers were overhead, but was unmoved by the sound of British planes.

BRUTUS

Pet of World War I flying ace Theodore Hammeker; he always accompanied him on sorties against the enemy.

CALVIN

A beloved cat of Charles Dudley Warner, American editor and essayist of the 19th century. A non-conformist cat.

CHANOINE

Victor Hugo's favourite cat. Huge and dignified, it sat on a red ottoman and received the homage of guests at the writer's literary gatherings.

CHARLES

Beloved pet of Michael Joseph, English publisher, cat-lover and author; also one very very large and stately Charles, owned by Rebecca Bone, whose speciality is finding very very small places to sleep in.

CHESSIE

A kitten used in the earliest advertising campaign for the Chesapeake Railroad.

CHIM

A demon cat drawn by Aubrey Beardsley for the romance *Sidonia and the Sorceress*.

DICK WHITTINGTON'S CAT

One of the most famous of cats whose name, however, has vanished in the mists of time.

EPLU

An American cat (1930s) owned by new settlers, so devoted to their country that they named the cat after the motto *E Pluribus Unum*.

FEATHERS

The pet of Carl van Vechten, author of *The Tiger In the House*.

FOSS | A cat who lived with Edward Lear, painter and beloved writer of children's nonsense poetry. Lear built his second house to an identical plan so that Foss would not have to adjust to a strange place.

F PUSS | A Parisian feline in whose care Ernest Hemingway used to leave his baby son. The writer, who had 30 cats in his Havana home, loved them for their 'absolute emotional honesty'.

HODGE | Dr Samuel Johnson's cat which James Boswell thought was treated far too well, for the goodly doctor would go and buy oysters for Hodge so the servants would not think him a nuisance. Mr Boswell, being allergic to cats, did not really approve.

JEOFFRY | Christopher Smart, an 18th-century English poet, was often in the mental asylum. A long excerpt from his most famous poem, 'I will consider my Cat Jeoffry' goes on to list all the things which make him wonderful.

KARE KEDI

The cat of psychic researcher Claude Farrere; Kare Kedi had a strange nervous fit at the same time that a devoted neighbour, a close friend, was being murdered.

SIR JOHN LANGBORN

A cat owned and 'knighted' by Jeremy Bentham; although lively and seductive when young, he grew so sedate and well-behaved in middle age that he was re-christened The Reverend Sir John Langborn. Bentham was an English jurist and reformer of the Georgian period.

LUDOVIC THE CRUEL

One of the 14 cats to whom Richelieu left a pension on his death. The French statesman and cardinal, virtual ruler of the country, signed death warrants while his cats sat on his lap.

MAHOMET'S CAT

The Prophet of Islam was known to be so attached to his pet that once, when he had to move, he cut off a piece of his gown rather than disturb her.

MELAMPYGE

As Jan Morris tells in 'Venetian Bestiary', when the 900-year-old great Campanile of San Marco collapsed in 1902 the only victim was the custodian's tabby cat, Melampyge.

MICETTO

A large grey cat, with black stripes, presented to Chateaubriand by Leo XII when the former was France's ambassador to the Vatican. Reared in a fold of the Pope's white robe, Micetto was accustomed to promenade daily on San Angelo's vast dome.

MINETTE

Pet of Gottfried Mind, the 'Raphael of Cats'. Rather than disturb her when she sat upon his knees, he would remain in the same position for hours.

MORRIS

A cat who appeared on TV in America in the 1970s for 9 Lives cat food and took the country by storm.

MOUTON

A well-loved French cat whose owner carved this verse on her tombstone:
'Ci repose pauvre Mouton
Qui jamais ne fût glouton;
J'espère bien que le roi Pluton
Lui donnera bon gîte et
    croûton.

MY LAI

Unhappy name for favourite cat of Ho Chi Minh.

MYSOUFF

Alexander Dumas' cat, who wandered around inconsolable when his master was late for dinner.

NINI

Nini lived in Venice in the late 19th century – a pampered café cat who became famous for the visitors who came to see him and signed the guest book; Verdi left a phrase or two from *La Traviata* as a memento.

OLIVER

One of a long series of cats who reigned over biologist Thomas Huxley's house. His punctuality at mealtimes was admirable, and his pertinacity in jumping on diners' shoulders until they gave him the best titbits indicated great firmness of purpose.

PADDINGTON

A large, fluffy brown cat, like a small bear; friend and companion of gardener and writer Sue Phillips. He appears every year on cards and notepaper.

PATTIPAWS

An Eliot cat; the names T.S. gave his real cats are much more sentimental than those of his fictional ones.

PEPPER-POT
SOOTIKINS
SCRATCH-AWAY

Three tabby kittens belonging to Thomas Hood, the poet.

PERRUQUE

Cardinal Richelieu's kitten who was born in the Marquis de Racan's wig, or perruque.

THE REVEREND
WENCESLAS
MUFF

Sir Roy Strong's cat, known to the world through his portrait by Martin Leman.

SHAN

White House Siamese; belonged to the daughter of Gerald Ford when he was president of US.

SLIPPERS

Theodore Roosevelt's pet cat who enjoyed protected status and immunity from the FBI.

TABBY

Abe Lincoln's not exactly unusual name for his pet.

TIDDLES

The Paddington cat. Adopted as a kitten by railwaymen at the London station, he had his own refrigerator stocked with steak, liver and other feline goodies. Not surprisingly, he grew to be London's biggest cat: 32 lb (14.5 kg) in weight and 30 in (75 cm) long.

TOM QUARTZ

A White House cat, so-named by Theodore Roosevelt after Mark Twain's tale of the Californian beast who had a 'cussed prejudice agin' quartz mining'.

TYBALT
CLARA

Pets of the writer Samuel Butler. Fonder of cats than he was of people, he was particularly passionate about the street cats of London.

WHITE HEATHER	Queen Victoria's remembrance of her beloved Scotland.
WILBERFORCE	The Downing Street cat who served under four British prime ministers. Policemen on guard duty were instructed to ring the front doorbell any time he wished to enter No. 10.
WILLIAM	Dickens' cat; re-christened Williamina when her sex had been established. She persisted in putting out the candle by which the writer was reading.
WINDY	The Flying Cat, owned by Wing Commander Gibson of the Royal Air Force.
WISCUS	Another of T.S. Eliot's cats, perhaps with long whiskers.
ZIZI	Silver-grey Angora, pet of the French novelist Théophile Gautier. She loved listening to music and occasionally picked her way along the keys of an open piano.
ZULEIKA	A cat with a snow-white breast, a member of Gautier's feline harem. He was often painted wearing Turkish costume and surrounded by cats.

LEGENDARY CATS

BASTET

The all-powerful Egyptian goddess of sexuality, the sun, the moon, virginity, good health, fertility; she was represented by a sitting cat. Bastet was also known as Pasht; some authorities believe that this is the derivation of the word 'puss'.

CHRISTIE

After the custom in Aix-en-Provence of wrapping the finest cat in the county in swaddling clothes on the feast of Corpus Christi. The animal was strewn with florets, and treated like a god. The tradition lasted until the 1750s.

DIANA

The virginal Greek goddess of the hunt, who turned herself into a cat and infuriated her fellow gods on Mount Olympus.

FREYA

The Norse goddess of love who chose a cat as her symbol – two black cats pulled her chariot.

GIB

After gibbe-cat, the medieval name for an old and serious animal, still used in northern England and Scotland; Falstaff describes himself as being, 'as melancholy as a Gib-cat'.

GRIMALKIN

The traditional name for a witch's cat, 'Grimalkin the foul Fiend', but also the name given to beloved family pets throughout medieval times. A cat called Grimalkin was mentioned by the naturalist Gilbert White as fostering a baby hare, continuing to play with and care for it even after the hare had grown up. A Grimalkin also appears in Shakespeare's *Macbeth*.

NOAH

After Noah, who built the Ark and saved all life from extinction in the flood; according to legend, cats were created at his express command.

PERSIANNA

After the Persians who, in about 500 BC, found a unique way to defeat the Egyptians. They were issued with a cat each and, as their enemy was forbidden to hurt or kill any cat, won the battle with ease. Surely a record for feline power. It is not suggested that the cats were Persian long-hairs.

RA

In the Egyptian Book of the Dead, Ra is pictured as a spotted cat, a recent development in modern cat breeding.

TSUN

A gentle white Birman, oracle of an old priest. She turned into a golden beast with the blue eyes of Tsun Kyanksie, Burmese goddess of the transmogrification of souls, when her owner was killed.

RECORD-BREAKING CATS

ARTHUR

Famous in Britain for appearing in a cat-food ad, this appealing white cat was fought over by two putative owners, and was said during the dispute to have taken refuge in the Russian Embassy – the only cat believed to have asked for asylum. (The Russian Embassy, after an investigation, cat-egorically denied the allegation).

CHARLIE CHAN

Only heir to the greatest fortune left to a cat: about $250,000 from a doting Missouri eccentric.

CHOUQUETTE

Waiting for new life in another century, Mme Olga Courtois deep-froze her dead cat in a specially designed catafalque, the only known feline in the science of cryogenics.

DUSTY

An American tabby who produced the US record at the time of 420 kittens.

FELIX

Cat who flew the equivalent of seven times around the world in the cargo hold of a Pan Am jet, clocking up nearly 180,000 miles and visiting 29 countries. Recaptured at Heathrow airport in London, she was treated to a champagne flight across the Atlantic to be reunited with her owners in Los Angeles.

HIMMY

An Australian cat who reached the world heavyweight record of 46 lb 15¼ oz (21.3 kg) in 1986.

JAZZ

This tabby cat was the only animal passenger on the R-34 – the first dirigible to cross the Atlantic from England to the United States.

JOCK

The only cat to attend War Cabinet meetings with his owner, Sir Winston Churchill. The Prime Minister was fond of cats and there was usually at least one in residence in Downing Street, spending more time in front of the fire and listening to political discussion rather than chasing mice.

JOSEPH	A very large tabby cat who weighed over 48 lb (22 kg).
MOUSTACHE	A soldier's cat, brave and dapper, who sat with the Belgian troops in World War I, watching the shells without ever being frightened.
NICKY	A suave Siamese who travelled the world with his diplomat owner. He lived in Budapest and Bangkok, New York and London, and died in Lagos, Nigeria.
SMUDGE	The only female member of the General, Municipal, Boilermakers and Allied Trades Union, Branch 29, in Scotland.
TIPPY	Highest record of a mother cat in Britain – 343 kittens.
TOWSER	Tortoiseshell cat with recorded mouse count of 25,029 as of 1986 – no doubt a nip or two in her home in a Scottish whisky distillery helped.

BLACK CATS

BLACKBERRY

A sweet purply-black fruit; the bush has thorns, so it is an appropriate name for a kitten with sharp claws.

BLACKCURRANT

Sharp, small and round; also rich in vitamin C, so a cat who is bouncy with good health!

BLACKGUARD

Not its most well-known meaning of a vagabond or criminal, but one of its original ones: a kitchen servant in a noble household; an appropriate name for a glutton of a cat who cleans up all the scraps in the kitchen.

BLACKJACK

The card game, for a gambolling kitten, or the weapon for a playful one, especially an animal who likes to jump up on your back without warning. Also for a rounded feline; a blackjack was a 16th-century leather-coated beer mug covered in tar.

BLACKOUT

Remember wartime regulations! For a really black black cat; if you can't see anything when its eyes are closed, then that's a Blackout Cat.

BLACKPOT

An old word for a beer mug, and for a heavy drinker, so any kitten who drinks more than the usual amount of milk or water.

BOWLER

These hats are usually black, round and smooth, so for a round and tumbly cat with a smooth coat.

BREW

From witch's brew, so a bubbly kitten apt to bring in toads and such.

CHARCOAL

Chunks of burnt wood; for a coat with faint brown striations.

CIMMERIAN

The Cimmerii were a legendary people said by the Greeks to live in perpetual darkness, so the word describes anything entirely dark; for a completely black cat with a dense, rather than silky, coat.

COALFACE

A black-faced puss. Also the place where the coal is cut, so the heart of the action, the front line. Perhaps for a cat who is always in the foreground of any trouble.

DOMINO

The enveloping black cloak worn at masquerades, sometimes with a half-mask; for a kitten who loves to play hide and seek. Also the black cloak worn by Dominican friars, so perhaps for a very serious cat.

EBON, EBONY EBONEOUS

A black wood used for inlay, sleek and dark; suitable for a short-haired cat with a subtle sheen to its coat.

GUTENBERG

From the first type in the German style known as Black Letter; appropriate for a very literary cat who enjoys playing with books and papers.

HAMLET

Always in a black suit; thereby hangs a tail . . .

INKSPOT

A blot of ink, also a famous quartet of black jazz singers; for a kitten who likes to swing.

JET

The source of much jewellery; for a sharp-faced kitten, with bright eyes that sparkle.

LAKKERLASS

Shiny pure black lacquer, for a very sleek female cat.

LIQUORICE

A favourite sweet of childhood.

LUCIFER

A fallen angel. For the sweetest-looking kitten with the most mischievous mind.

MARIA

The Black Maria (with the accent on the i) is the slang word for the prison van sent out at night to collect offenders from the streets. Perhaps for a cat who is always moving her kittens around.

MIDNIGHT

The middle of the night, the blackest of blackness, for a totally black cat with no white.

NOCTURNE

Night music: for a sweetly tuned miaow in the night.

ODILE

The Black Swan in *Swan Lake*; not so much wicked as enchanted by the Magician – and endlessly seductive.

OTHELLO

The great Moor warrior of Venice, immortalized by Shakespeare, and always played as a large, imposing, quiet but effective character. The perfect name for a brave and essentially kind feline.

PITCH

Black as pitch – a really, really black cat!

PLUTO   King of the Underworld.

SLOEBERRY   A small black plum used in
                     making wine and gin; for an
                     undersized kitten, with a good
                     punch or batting paw.

THUNDER   A proverbial cat, black as
                     thunder.

ZOMBI   A name invented by the poet
                     Robert Southey for a young,
                     frightened kitten which
                     vanished into the cellar and
                     was never seen in the day. For
                     a night prowler of a cat!

WHITE CATS

ALABASTER

White quartz, slightly transparent, with a clouded look. Used a great deal for funeral urns and monuments, so especially for a very stately, short-haired cat, quiet and sombre in character.

ALBINESSA

The feminine of albino; a ghost of a cat, with pale eyes.

BANQUO

Because his ghost was white; a cat who appears without a sound.

BIANCA

Italian name for white; also Katherine's sister in *The Taming of the Shrew*. With the lovely song about Bianca in the Cole Porter score of *Kiss Me Kate*, any cat could feel happy with such a name.

BLANCO

Whitening cream used by the armed services. Appropriate for a general of a cat, startlingly white, who always looks neat and tidy.

BOURBON

Not the whiskey, but the white flag of the Bourbon kings of France, the antithesis of the red flags of revolutionary Europe. Obviously for a cat of regal demeanour.

CISTERCIAN

The white monks, from the undyed wool of their habits. For a serious kitten who likes to meditate on the strange occurrences of life.

CREAMPUFF

The image of a roly-poly long-haired kitten who is also a softy at heart.

CRYSTAL

A name for a blue-white Persian kitten with blue eyes, all glitter and shine.

CUE BALL

The white ball in snooker; for a kitten who loves rolling around on the floor chasing balls.

ERMINE

The most royal of furs, flatter than white fox or white mink, but indefinably more elegant. A surprise that it is in fact the winter coat of the common stoat, whose Latin name is the Armenian mouse. Why shouldn't a cat be named after a mouse...

FLAKE

Flake white is the traditional white pigment of the artist; suitable also for trendier cat-owners who find they have an off-the-wall cat.

FOOLSCAP   A longer-than-normal sheet of
                paper, so for a seriously literate
                cat, perhaps even a judicious
                one: most lawyers' notes are
                written on foolscap.

FROSTY   Sparkling; a bright cheerful
                purr on a cold morning.

GHOST   The shadow of a silent
                miaow...

KYOTO   Kyoto, Japan. In the year 999,
                a white cat belonging to the
                Emperor Ichijo gave birth to
                five pure-white kittens, so
                precious that they were cared
                for as if they were princesses.
                They are believed to be the first
                pure-bred white cats.

LILYWHITE

A virtue as well as a colour; for a goody-goody cat? Perhaps one with a habit of looking smug.

MARSHMALLOW

Round and sticky, and very difficult to pick off almost any surface; for a kitten who clings to your back and refuses to let go.

MILKY

A healthy name for a vitamin-filled, energetic and bouncy, happy cat.

NIVEOUS

Resembling snow. Imagine a fresh fall of soft flakes – obviously a long-haired pile of white fur.

ODETTE

The White Swan in *Swan Lake*, symbol of purity and goodness. Sounds too good to be true.

PAVLOVA

The famous ballet dancer. Especially suitable for an Australian cat – Pavlova is also a white meringue dessert.

PERSIL

Whiter than white! For a sparkling kitten, pure white without a shadow of a stain!

PORCELEENA

The finest white china; for an oriental cat with thin bones and translucent coat.

PUFFBALL

A large white mushroom, so a lovely round and fluffy cat.

RINSO

Famous soap powder. For a whiter than white cat; especially appropriate for one with a high voice: Beverly Sills, the soprano, began her career as a child singing the Rinso White commercial.

SNOW-WHITE

Walt Disney's greatest role-model for little girls.

VANILLA

The essence is deep brown, but the scent is surely pure white – delicate and delicious, and, in spite of all the novel ice cream flavours, still everybody's favourite. Just right for a kitten who loves watching the oven when there's cooking going on.

WHITEWASH

Lime wash for walls; slightly mottled. For a slightly shady cat! Also a cover-up; perhaps liberating a little fish from the platter with one paw, but continuing to wash the other quite, quite innocently...

GINGER CATS

BLONDIE

The long-suffering wife of Dagwood in the American cartoon strip. Just the name for an animal that is a strawberry blonde shade of ginger – even though few cats are long-suffering.

BUTTERCUP

A pale, pure shade of gold for a pale, pure cat that looks as though butter wouldn't melt in its mouth.

COPPER

For a dark, red-ginger animal. Alchemists believed that the metal was the symbol of Venus, so ... the name for a loving, or even lovelorn, cat.

GINGERBREAD

A sweet, spicy cake, so the ideal name for a sweet-natured animal with just a touch of mischief. It also means unsubstantial wares that are intrinsically worthless, but that could never apply to a cat.

GINGERSNAP

A sweet, brittle biscuit flavoured with ginger – or a person who is easily irritated. For a generally affectionate cat of unpredictable temper.

MANDARIN

A vibrantly orange citrus fruit, but also a pompous bureaucrat. Just right for a startlingly ginger cat who insists on everything being just so.

MARIGOLD

Deep orange flowers, named after the Virgin Mary. They stand erect with their faces turned to the sun – just like a cat on the first warm day of spring.

MARMALADE

A bitter-sweet breakfast preserve, a delicious deep orange blend of chunky fruit and syrup. Best for a cat with an ascerbic edge to its personality.

PLANTAGENET

England's most exciting dynasty took its name from a sprig of golden broom, and recumbent lions, close relative of the cat, decorated its banners and shields. For a regal animal, more gold than ginger.

SAFFRON

An orange-yellow flavouring, subtle but unmistakable. For a cat of unique character and quiet determination.

SUNSHINE

The colour of a truly ginger cat.

GREY CATS

BLUEY

For a feline – ideally an Australian one – that's a bluish shade of grey.

CHARLES

After the second Earl Grey, who abolished slavery throughout the British Empire in 1833.

CHIAROSCURO

Painting in light and dark shades: suitable for a cat that combines almost white and nearly black greys in its coat.

EMINENCE

Père Joseph, whose policy and influence inspired Richelieu, was called the Grey Eminence because he was a shadowy figure behind the cardinal. For a cat who's not much in evidence, but who nevertheless rules his household.

GRISAILLE

A technique of painting in shades of grey. A subtle name for a cat whose coat runs the gamut from smoke to charcoal grey.

JANE

After Lady Jane Grey, who was queen of England for just ten days before she was imprisoned and executed.

CALICO CATS

CALICUT
Once the great emporium of northern India, one of the chief trading posts with Europe, which gave its name to calico fabric.

CHECKERS
Board game played with coloured marbles – for a cat who likes to play with balls.

CHUKWA
The tortoise who, according to Hindu legend, supports the elephant Maha-pudma, who in turn supports the world. For a sturdy cat with tortoiseshell markings.

CRAZY PAVING
Irregular patterns of stone, for a garden-loving cat who likes to lie on the warm paving.

CRAZY QUILT
Patches of all colours, for a colourful cat who is not necessarily crazy.

FRECKLES
Obvious connotation; a cat with smaller patches than usual dotted all over its coat.

MANEKI NEKO
Japanese good luck cat of three colours, meaning 'beckoning cat' because traditionally her waving paw warned her mistress of danger.

MOTLEY	The multi-coloured attire worn by medieval jesters . . . so a happy-go-lucky calico cat.
PINTO	A kind of pony, small and very fast, with splashes of colour – for a speedy cat.
PIPER	After the Pied Piper; pied also means mottled; a special name for a cat good at catching rats.
SPANGLE	Yet another word for mottled, but this time much prettier.
TESS	From tesserae, small glass or clay mosaics. For a cat with small patches in many different colours.
TOMMY	A bonny tortoiseshell cat with a red morocco collar, who came to an untimely end: he was sat upon by a visiting deacon and crushed to death.
TRIAD	A three-tone chord in music. Also a Chinese secret society, so it's an appropriate name for a calico cat with white and oriental parents.
TRICORNE	Three-cornered hat – so give the name to a calico cat with a black splash on its head.

TABBY CATS

FELIS

BENGAL

After the Bengal tiger – a fearsome beast; also the name of a famous British regiment. Ideal for a dedicated hunter.

DIDO

A tabby cat that belonged to Robert Southey, the Poet Laureate.

ESSO

From the advertisement for petrol, advising motorists to put a tiger in their tanks – a striped cat.

GOSSIP

Tabby used to mean a chattering woman – just the name for a talkative cat.

LORENZO

After Lorenzo Lotto, one of the few Venetian painters to include a tabby cat in a painting – *The Annunciation* (*c.* 1527).

TABBY

Tabby is the name of a brownish-grey, striped watered silk named for the Baghdad neighbourhood where it was made (Atabis). Only later (1665) applied to cats with similar markings.

TABITHA	Aramaic word for gazelle; also Puritan name. Mistaken for a nickname for tabby as in cat and so has become a common name for a cat in children's stories.
TAFFETA	A crisp, lustrous fabric with a watered pattern was known as tabby in France; for a cat with shimmering markings.
THOMAS	The common name for a tom, especially a tabby tom; also 'beautiful Tom Cat', a mouser who was left on his own by Widow Tomkins without food and ate himself up bit by bit.
TIBBET	Family which had a mountain tabby cat as a heraldic charge, an obvious combination of the common word for tabby and the family name.
TIGER	The natural name for a small striped cat.
TROTSKY	Why not?
ZEBRA ZEBRINA	A dark-striped pussy, perhaps with yellow eyes.

LONG-HAIRED CATS

ANKARA

The capital of Turkey, and birthplace of long-haired Angora cats. Ankara was known as Angora until 1930.

CHRISTMAS

For a cat with tipping on its coat: just like the powdered artificial snow used to dress Christmas trees.

COLETTE

For the writer whose stories of Cheri make cats look clumsy in comparison to the silky elegance of her characters.

CUPID

The Christian name of the first recorded cream Persian, in the late 19th century. Also the Roman god of love – so use it for an amorous feline.

ELINOR

Elinor Glyn's *Three Weeks* shocked the world in 1907. She herself firmly believed that a half-undressed woman and a luxuriously long-haired cat stretched out on a tigerskin rug were the images of erotica that every man dreamed of.

ENTRECHAT

The ballet step done with immeasurable grace. Suitable for Persians, or other long-haired cats, with their lithe, almost silent, movements.

HARDY	Although Persians look effete, they are among the hardiest of cats – feline counterparts of Pekinese dogs whose tiny size belies their immense courage.
KHOMEINI	Religious leader who ousted the Shah of Iran and instituted an Islamic republic. For a grimly determined cat.
LAMBKIN	Silver Lambkin was the result of a meeting between a chinchilla and a nondescript stray. His stuffed body is in the Natural History Museum in London.
OMAR KHAYYAM	The Persian poet, astronomer and mathematician, known for his *Rubáiyát*, a collection of verses popularized by Edward Fitzgerald's translation in the 19th century.
SHAH	The ancient ruler of Persia, now Iran. For an imperious cat who rules his human family with a rod of iron.
SORAYA	A former empress of Iran, sloe-eyed and glamorous – for a sloe-eyed and glamorous Persian cat.

STIRLING

For a brown long-haired cat after B.A. Stirling, who bred the first pedigree one in England.

YILDIZCEK
YILDIZ

The first official Angoras to arrive in America, by courtesy of the governor of Ankara in 1963.

ABYSSINIAN CATS

AMBER — A sparklingly translucent, yellow-brown resin used for jewellery. Together with hazel and green, it is just the colour of a true Abyssinian's eyes.

BUNNY — A strange name for a cat, but Abyssinians are sometimes called bunny cats because their fur is like that of a rabbit.

CARTER — After Howard Carter, the Egyptologist who excavated the tomb of Chnemhetep which, in its decoration, shows a cat that looks just like the modern Abyssinian breed.

CLEOPATRA — The queen of Egypt who enchanted both Julius Caesar and Mark Antony. Abyssinians closely resemble ancient Egyptian cats, and they are, of course, enchanting ...

JUDAH — After Haile Selassie, the late lion of Judah and emperor of Abyssinia (now Ethiopia). For a regal cat.

ZULA — The first Abyssinian cat in Britain, introduced by Lord Robert Napier, whose military expedition to Abyssinia landed at the port of Zula.

SIAMESE CATS

ANNA

After the English governess in *The King and I*, who took control of the Siamese royal family – just as a Siamese cat rules over a household.

BANGKOK

Capital of Thailand (originally Siam), home of Siamese cats. They first came to Britain in the late 19th century.

BING

Because Siamese cats croon, just like the Old Groaner himself.

CHAMPAGNE

The palest shade on a seal point Siamese's coat.

ENG
CHANG

The original Siamese twins, discovered in Mekong in Siam in 1829 when they were about 15 years old. For a pair of cats who are almost inseparable.

GAN SU

A city near the Gobi desert; suitable for a sand-colour Siamese, like a pale cream point.

HO CHI MINH

The Terror of the Neighbourhood; for an aggressive fighter who slinks in and out of the jungle.

LYCHEE

A delicious fruit, white and creamy inside with a crisp brown coat; for a cream or seal point Siamese.

MAO TSE-TUNG

Big Boss; a large and inscrutable Siamese.

SAWARSDEE

The Siamese word for hello ... so, a cat that's constantly talking.

SUKHOTHAI

Capital of ancient Siam kingdom.

SUN YAT SEN

The most westernized of modern Chinese leaders, wise and diplomatic.

THAI-BREAKER

A Siamese cat who likes looking at tennis matches on television.

THAI-DYE

An obvious but delightful pun on the modern name for Siam.

THAI-FOON

A cat who rushes through the house like a hurricane.

YUL

He played the King of Siam in *The King and I*; in a bald head, true, and there are few bald Siamese, but with that bony face and wide forehead ...

BURMESE CATS

CHARTREUSE — A yellow liqueur, made in France from a delicious mixture of herbs and flowers – and just the colour of a brown Burmese's eyes.

CHOCOLADO — From the soft, seal-brown fur of the original Burmese, first introduced into Britain in the 1950s and the United States in 1930.

DODGER — From the Artful Dodger, star pupil of the school for thieves in Charles Dickens' *Oliver Twist*. Burmese have been seen to open doors, cupboards and even refrigerators in order to reach their favourite food.

GOON — From Rangoon, the capital of Burma. Also the title of one of Britain's ever-popular comedy radio shows. For a clownish type of cat.

MANDY — From Mandalay, the Burmese city that features in the song *On the Road to Mandalay*. The playing flying fishes that it refers to would be heaven for any cat.

MONSOON — The rain-bearing wind that drenches Burma – and the rest of Southeast Asia – every summer. Perhaps for a cat that revels in a downpour.

RINA — From ballerina because, like dancers, Burmese cats move with grace and elegance – and know how to use their muscles.

SAGAPOR — The Greek word meaning 'I love you'. Burmese, like other oriental cats, make a great show of loving. Unlike the Greeks bearing gifts, they generally mean it.

WEDGIE — Not after the British politician Anthony Wedgwood Benn, whose nickname this is, but because of the shape of a Burmese's face: like a wedge, with a rounded head and large ears.

WONG MAU — The first Burmese cat in the West, brought to the United States in 1930.

YANKEE — Because, like the American troops who took Britain by storm during World War II, the Burmese were instantly popular.

MANX CATS

LOST PROPERTY BOX

BONHAKI

A silver tabby, the breed's first champion in England in the early 1900s. Edward VII owned several Manx cats.

CHEEKY

Not a reference to a Manx's character – although it can be as cheeky as any other cat – but to the shape of its head: the cheeks should be prominent.

DOUGLAS

After the capital of the Isle of Man, said to be the birthplace of Manx cats. For a wealthy cat – the island is a tax haven.

ESPAÑA

According to legend, a tailless breed of cat was carried on one of the ships from the Spanish Armada which was wrecked on the Isle of Man after defeat by Sir Francis Drake in 1558.

MIXER

Another legend says that Manx cats are the result of a cat mating with a rabbit.

MONA

The ancient Roman name for the Isle of Man. Yet another legend about the origin of these mysterious cats says that a tailless puss swam from Noah's ark on Ararat to an islet off the island.

RUMPY

The lack of which is no doubt the reason for this nickname.

SPHINX

Like Egypt's famous statue – half woman and half lion – the Manx cat is shrouded in mystery: its origins, still unknown, were possibly in Asia or Japan.

TEE-TEE

After the motor cycle race held on the Isle of Man each year. For a speedy cat who moves purposefully around the house.

WALKER

Because Manx cats take well to a collar and lead – making them ideal for owners who like their pets to take them for a walk but prefer cats to dogs.

RUSSIAN BLUES

ALMOND

The shape of a Russian Blue's vivid green eyes.

ANASTASIA

The daughter of Russia's last tsar, Nicholas II, who may or may not have been executed by Bolsheviks in 1918. For an enigmatic cat, of uncertain – but definitely Russian – ancestry.

ARCHANGEL

The name for Russian Blues before 1900. They were brought to Britain by sailors from the port of Archangel in what is now the Soviet Union.

BAA-BAA

Because one of these cats was exchanged for a leg of mutton by a Russian sailor from a ship trading between the Baltic and northern Britain.

BOLSHOI

After Russia's Bolshoi Ballet. Unlike ballet dancers, the cats are quiet in temperament and behaviour.

BORIS, SOPHIA
TATIANA

More Russian names.

BORODIN

After the Russian composer whose cats 'marched back and forth on the table ... leaping on the backs of guests'.

CATHERINE

After Catherine the Great, empress of Russia, who increased her empire at the cost of Turkey, Sweden and Poland. Just the name for a female cat who invades other cats' territories.

IVAN

After Ivan the Terrible, grand duke of Muscovy, and the first tsar of Russia in the 16th century. Also a popular Russian name, so ideal for a popular cat.

MICHAEL

One of the archangels of medieval theology; Russian Blues were originally from Archangel.

MIKHAIL

After Mikhail Gorbachev, leader of the Soviet Union. For a cat who knows that there is a world outside his immediate territory.

TSAR, TSARINA

The emperor of Russia and his empress. Just right for an autocratic beast (as most cats are).

JUST CATS

AUBREY

For an animal of wicked temperament. Aubrey Beardsley drew demonic black cats; four of his drawings illustrate Poe's *Tales of Mystery and Wonder*.

AUGUSTUS

A large and lazy cat.

CANDIDE

Hero of Voltaire's satirical novel, who travelled the world before deciding that it was best to cultivate one's own back garden. For a travelling cat who always – eventually – returns home.

CATMANDU

A serene cat from the mountains of happiness.

CHAIRMAN MIAOW

A boss cat without a red book.

CHARLIE CHAN

From the famous San Francisco detective – a clever cat indeed.

CHESTERFIELD

The fourth earl of Chesterfield, English statesman and writer, left pensions for life to his cats and their offspring. A good example to his own heir, whom he smothered with advice in *Letters to His Son* (1774).

CLEMENTINE	After the black cat of St Clement Dane church in London who delighted in climbing the organ pipes to enjoy a solitary concert.
CUSTARD	From 'Cat and Custard Pot' inn signs – and cats, of course, do like to lick up the remains of this delicious sauce.
DOMENICO	In Domenico Ghirlandaio's fresco of *The Last Supper*, painted in the 15th century, a cat of high intelligence scowls at the arch-traitor Judas.
DON JUAN	For a very lecherous cat.
FELICITY	From Felic, the language of cats; unlike dogs, who communicate only with vowel sounds, they also use at least six consonants.
GATTO	Italian for cat.
HEP CAT	For a lively cat who might like to dance!
HOKUSAI	After the Japanese artist whose coloured prints of cats reveal all their charm, grace and essential mystery.

HULA

After the hula hoop that's whirled around the body when waist and hips move fast enough; for a tail-chasing cat that seems to form itself into a permanent circle.

ISAAC

The scientist and philosopher Isaac Newton had two holes cut in his door: a large one for his cat and a smaller opening for her kittens.

JEZEBEL

From the biblical lady who encouraged idolatry and met a sticky end, but generally used for any schemer who entices men to evil-doing. So for a flirtatious cat, perhaps?

LUCA

In Luca Giordano's 18th-century painting of the birth of the Virgin the only chair in the room is occupied by a serenely sleeping cat, ignoring the great event.

MACKINTOSH

From the Mackintosh of Mackintosh, chief of the Highland clan whose motto is: 'Touch not the cat except with a glove.' For a fierce and untouchable Scottish cat.

PETERKIN

For a cat with a loud and cheerful voice; from Cicely Hamilton's poem: '"The Lord likes cheerful noises" says Peterkin, the cat!... Prrrrrraise!'

PEWTER

From the pewter pots of various sizes used to measure drinks in pubs. Stealing these was known as 'cat and kitten sneaking'.

POSTIE

After all the cats who have worked for the British Post Office, and been on its payroll, since 1868, when complaints that mail was being destroyed by rats and mice led to the employment of cats at 1s a week – now raised to £1.

PUDDLES

For a cat who positively enjoys getting wet – some felines have been known to swim and hunt in lakes and rivers, others are trained to dive for fish.

ROBESPIERRE

A cat with a penchant for ordering others about; after the 'sea-green incorruptible' of the French Revolution.

SCARLATTI

Alessandro Scarlatti's 'Cat Fugue' was inspired by his pet strolling on the keyboard of his harpsichord. At the climax of the piece, the cat 'swells to a tiger'.

SID

For a cat who is always just out of sight, after the leading – but invisible – character in advertisements for the privatization of British Gas.

SOUR-PUSS

For a sulky cat.

SVENGALI

After the Hungarian musician who mesmerized Trilby O'Ferrall in the novel by George du Maurier – because cats, too, mesmerize their owners.

TANKER

The insignia of the US Tank Corp in World War I was a huge black cat with fangs and flashing green eyes. The corp's motto, 'Treat 'em rough', is not recommended for cats.

VALERIAN

A herb used to make a sedative for humans – but with a kick like champagne for cats. Just right for a fizzy, bubbly, extrovert beast.

WABASHA

After the cats on the staff of the Anderson House Hotel in Wabasha, Minnesota, who are hired as companions for an hour, an evening, or overnight.

WAIN (OR WAYNE)

The artist Louis Wain drew rakish London alley cats, smoking cigars and riding motor cycles.

WILLOW

From pussy willow, with its delicate, silvery catkins.

WOLSEY

Cardinal Thomas Wolsey, Henry VIII's lord chancellor, took his cat with him to the council chamber, where it sat by his side during the long and weary proceedings.

YO YO

A spool attached to a piece of string, which rises and falls as the string is manipulated; for a cat that's always jumping up and down.

INDEX

Abyssinia, 66
Abyssinian cats, 65-6
Aesop, 11
Aix-en-Provence, 31
Alabaster, 45
Albinessa, 45
alchemy, 51
Almond, 77
Amber, 66
Anastasia, 77
Anderson House Hotel,
    Wabasha, 85
Angora cats, 62, 64
Ankara, 62, 64
Anna, 68
Ararat, 74
Archangel, 77, 78
Aristo-Cats, 11
Armada, 74
Artful Dodger, 71
Arthur, 35
Asia, 75
Asparagus, 11
Atlantic Ocean, 36
Aubrey, 80
Augustus, 80
Australia, 36, 48

Baa-Baa, 77
Baghdad, 59
Baltic, 77
Bangkok, 37, 68
Banquo, 45
Bastet, 31
Beardsley, Aubrey, 22, 80
Beelzebub, 21

Belaud, 21
Bellcat, 11
Bengal, 59
Benn, Anthony Wedgwood, 72
Bentham, Jeremy, 24
Bentley, Nicolas, 11
Beppo, 21
Bianca, 45
Bible, 82
Bing, 68
Bismarck, 21
black cats, 38-43
Black Maria, 42
Blackberry, 39
Blackcurrant, 39
Blackguard, 39
Blackjack, 39
Blackout, 39
Blackpot, 40
Blanco, 45
Blatherskit, 21
Blondie, 51
Bluey, 54
Bolshoi, 77
Bomber, 21
Bone, Rebecca, 22
Bonhaki, 74
Boris, 77
Borodin, 77
Borodin, Alexander, 77
Boswell, James, 23
Bourbon, 45
Bowler, 40
Breakfast at Tiffany's, 12
Brew, 40
British Gas, 84

Brutus, 21
Budapest, 37
Buffalo Bill, 21
Bulwer-Lytton, 14
Bunny, 66
Burma, 33, 72
Burmese cats, 70-2
Bustopher Jones, 11
Butler, Samuel, 28
Buttercup, 51
Byron, Lord, 21

calico cats, 55-7
Calicut, 56
Calvin, 21
Candide, 80
Capote, Truman, 12
Capri, 13
Carroll, Lewis, 12
Carter, 66
Carter, Howard, 66
Cat, 12
Catherine, 78
Catherine the Great, Empress
   of Russia, 78
Catmandu, 80
Cats, 11, 16
Chairman Miaow, 80
Champagne, 68
Chang, 68
Chanoine, 22
Charcoal, 40
Charles, 22, 54
Charlie Chan, 35, 80
Chartreuse, 71
Chateaubriand, Vicomte de,
   25
Checkers, 56

Cheeky, 74
Chesapeake Railroad, 22
Cheshire Cat, 12
Chessie, 22
Chesterfield, 80
Chesterfield, 4th Earl of, 80
Chiaroscuro, 54
Chim, 22
Chnemhetep, 66
Chocolado, 71
Chouquette, 35
Christie, 31
Christmas, 62
Chukwa, 56
Churchill, Sir Winston, 36
Cimmerian, 40
Cimmerii, 40
Cistercian, 46
Clara, 28
Clementine, 81
Cleopatra, 66
Coalface, 40
Colette, 62
Copper, 51
Corpus Christi, feast of, 31
Courtois, Olga, 35
Crazy Paving, 56
Crazy Quilt, 56
Creampuff, 46
Crystal, 46
Cue Ball, 46
Cupid, 62
Custard, 81

Dagwood, 51
Diana, 31
Dick Whittington's cat, 22
Dickens, Charles, 15, 29, 71

Dido, 59
Dinah, 12
Disney, Walt, 11, 49
Disraeli, 21
Dodger, 71
Domenico, 81
Dominicans, 41
Domino, 41
Don Juan, 81
Douglas, 74
Downing Street, 29, 36
Drake, Sir Francis, 74
Du Bellay, Joachim, 21
Du Maurier, George, 84
Dumas, Alexandre, 26
Dusty, 35

Ebon, 41
Eboneous, 41
Ebony, 41
Edward VII, King of England, 74
Egypt, 31, 32, 33, 66, 75
Elinor, 62
Eliot, T.S., 11, 14, 15, 16, 18, 27, 29
Eminence, 54
Eng, 68
Entrechat, 62
Eplu, 22
Ermine, 46
Espana, 74
Esso, 59
Ethiopia, 66

F Puss, 23
Falstaff, 31
famous cats, 20-9

Farrere, Claude, 24
FBI, 28
Feathers, 22
Felic, 81
Felicity, 81
Felissa, 12
Felix, 12, 18, 36
Fitzgerald, Edward, 63
Flake, 46
Foolscap, 47
Ford, Gerald, 28
Foss, 23
France, 45, 60
Francois, 12
Freckles, 56
French Revolution, 84
Freya, 31
Frosty, 47

Gallico, Paul, 14
Gallop, 12
Gan Su, 68
Gatto, 81
Gautier, Théophile, 29
General, Municipal, Boilermaker and Allied Trades Union, 37
George, W.L., 15
Ghirlandaio, Domenico, 81
Ghost, 47
Gib, 13, 31
Gibson, Wing-Commander, 29
ginger cats, 50-2
Gingerbread, 51
Gingersnap, 51
Giordano, Luca, 82
Gladstone, 21
Glyn, Elinor, 62

Gobi desert, 68
Goon, 71
Gorbachev, Mikhail, 78
Gossip, 59
Grand-ville, 17
Gray, Thomas, 17
Greece, 31, 72
Grey, Earl, 54
Grey, Lady Jane, 54
grey cats, 53-4
Grimalkin, 15, 32
Grisaille, 54
Growltiger, 13
Gus the Theatre Cat, 11
Gutenberg, 41

Haile Selassie, Emperor, 66
Hale, Katherine, 16
Hamilton, Cicely, 83
Hamlet, 41
Hammeker, Theodore, 21
Hardy, 63
Heathrow airport, 36
Hemingway, Ernest, 23
Henry VIII, King of England, 85
Hep Cat, 81
Hiddigeigei, 13
Himmy, 36
Hindus, 56
Ho Chi Minh, 26, 68
Hodge, 23
Hokusai, 81
Hood, Thomas, 27
Horatio, 81
Hugo, Victor, 22
Hula, 82
Hurlyburly-Buss, 13

Huxley, Thomas, 27

Ichijo, Emperor, 47
India, 56
Inkspot, 41
Iran, 63
Irving, Sir Henry, 11
Isaac, 82
Isle of Man, 74-5
Italy, 81
Ivan the Terrible, 78

Jacobina, 14
Jane, 54
Japan, 47, 56, 75, 81
Jazz, 36
Jennie, 14
Jennyanydots, 14
Jeoffry, 23
Jet, 41
Jezebel, 82
Jock, 36
Johnson, Samuel, 23
Joseph, 37
Joseph, Michael, 22
Joseph, Père, 54
Judah, 66
Judas, 81
Julius Caesar, 66

Kallicrates, 15
Kare Kedi, 24
Khomeini, 63
The King and, I, 68, 69
Kiss Me Kate, 45
Kyoto, 47

La Fontaine, Jean de, 17

Lady Jane, 15
Lagos, 37
Lakkerlass, 41
Lambkin, 63
Langborn, Sir John, 24
Lear, Edward, 23
legendary cats, 30-3
Leman, Martin, 27
Leo XII, Pope, 25
Lilywhite, 48
Lincoln, Abraham, 28
Liquorice, 42
literary cats, 10-18
Lloyd Webber, Andrew, 11
London, 27, 37, 81
long-haired cats, 61-4
Lorenzo, 59
Los Angeles, 36
Loti, Pierre, 18
Lotto, Lorenzo, 59
Luca, 82
Lucifer, 42
Ludovic the Cruel, 24
Lychee, 69

Macavity, 15
Mackintosh, 82
Maha-pudma, 56
Mahomet's Cat, 24
Malkin, 15
Mandalay, 71
Mandarin, 52
Mandy, 71
Maneki Neko, 56
Manx cats, 73-5
Mao Tse Tung, 69
Maria, 42
Marigold, 52

Mark Antony, 66
Marmalade, 52
Marquis, Don, 15, 17
Marriage, Caroline, 17
Marshmallow, 48
Mary, Virgin, 52, 82
Mehitabel, 15
Mekong, 68
Melampyge, 25
Micetto, 25
Michael, 78
Midnight, 42
Mikhail, 78
Milky, 48
Mind, Gottfried, 26
Minette, 26
Minnaloushe, 15
Miss Tabby, 16
Mr. Mistoffelees, 16
Mixer, 74
Mona, 74
Monsoon, 72
Morris, 26
Morris, Jan, 25
Motley, 57
Moustache, 37
Mouton, 26
Mungojerrie, 16
Munro, H.H., 18
My Lai, 26
Mysouff, 26

Napier, Lord Robert, 66
Natural History Museum,
  London, 63
Nelson, Lord, 81
New York, 37
Newton, Isaac, 82

Nicholas II, Tsar, 77
Nicky, 37
Nigeria, 37
Nightingale, Florence, 21
Nini, 26
Niveous, 48
Noah, 32, 74
Nocturne, 42
Norsemen, 31

Odile, 42
Old Deuteronomy, 16
*Old Possum's Book of
Practical Cats*, 11, 13, 15,
16, 18
Oliver, 27
Olympus, Mount, 31
Omar Khayyam, 63
On the Road to Mandalay, 71
Orlando, 16
Osborn, Paul, 18
Othello, 42

Paddington, 27
Paddington Station, 28
Pan Am, 36
Pasht, 31
Pattipaws, 27
Pavlova, 48
Pepper-Pot, 27
Percy, 17
Perdita, 17
Perrault, 17
Perruque, 27
Persia, 32
Persian cats, 62-3
Persianna, 32
Persil, 48

Peterkin, 83
Pewter, 83
Phillips, Sue, 27
Pied Piper, 57
Pinto, 57
Piper, 57
Pitch, 43
Plantagenet, 52
Pluto, 17, 43
Poe, Edgar Allan, 17, 80
Poland, 78
Porceleena, 49
Porter, Cole, 45
Post Office, 83
Postie, 83
Potter, Beatrix, 18
Puddles, 83
Puffball, 49
Puritans, 60
Puss in Boots, 17
Pyewacket, 17

R-34, 36
Ra, 33
Racan, Marquis de, 27
Raminagrobis, 17
Rangoon, 71
Ravenscroft, 13
record-breaking cats, 34-7
Reverend Wenceslas Muff, 27
Richelieu, Cardinal, 24, 27, 54
Rina, 72
Rinso, 49
Robespierre, 84
Romans, 74
Roosevelt, Theodore, 28
Rumpel-Stizchen, 13
Rumpelteazer, 16

Rumpy, 75
Russia, 35
Russian cats, 76-8

Saffron, 52
Sagapor, 72
St. Clement Dane, London, 81
Saki, 18
San Francisco, 80
Sawarsdee, 69
Scarlatti, 84
Scarlatti, Alessandro, 84
Scheffel, Joseph Victor von, 13
Scratch-Away, 27
Selima, 17
Shah, 63
Shakespeare, William, 32, 42, 45
Shan, 28
Siamese cats, 67-9
Sid, 84
Sills, Beverly, 49
Simkins, 18
Skimble-Shanks, 18
Slippers, 28
Sloeberry, 43
Smart, Christopher, 23
Smith, Stevie, 12
Smudge, 37
Snow-White, 49
Sootikins, 27
Sophia, 77
Soraya, 63
Sour Puss, 84
Southeast Asia, 72
Southey, Robert, 13, 43, 59
Soviet Union, 77
Spangle, 57

Spanish Armada, 74
Sphinx, 75
Stirling, 64
Stirling, B.A., 64
Strong, Sir Roy, 27
Sukhothai, 69
Sullivan, Pat, 12
Sun Yat Sen, 69
Sunshine, 52
Susie Wong, 18
Svengali, 84
Swan Lake, 42
Sweden, 78
Sylvester, 18

Tabby, 28, 59
tabby cats, 58-60
Tabitha, 60
Taffeta, 60
Tanker, 84
Tatiana, 77
Tee-Tee, 75
Tess, 57
Thai-Breaker, 69
Thai-Dye, 69
Thai-Foon, 69
Thailand, 68
Thomas, 60
Thunder, 43
Tibbet, 60
Tiddles, 28
Tiger, 60
Tippy, 37
Tobermory, 18
Tom, 18
Tom Cat, 60
Tom Quartz, 28
Tomkins, Widow, 60

Tommy, 57
Towser, 37
Triad, 57
Tricorne, 57
Trotsky, 60
Tsar, 78
Tsarina, 78
Tsun, 33
Tsun Kyanksie, 33
Turiri, 18
Turkey, 62, 78
Twain, Mark, 21, 28
Tybalt, 28

US Tank Corp, 84

Valerian, 85
Van Druten, John, 17
Vanilla, 49
Vatican, 25
Vechten, Carl van, 13, 22
Venice, 25, 26, 42
Venus, 51
Verdi, Giuseppe, 26
Victoria, Queen of England, 29
Virgin Mary, 52, 82
Voltaire, 80

Wabasha, 85
Wain, 85
Wain, Louis, 85
Walker, 75
War Cabinet, 36
Warner, Charles Dudley, 21

Wayne, 85
Wedgie, 72
white cats, 44-9
White, Gilbert, 32
White Heather, 29
White House, 28
Whitewash, 49
Whittington, Dick, 22
Wilberforce, 29
William, 29
Williamina, 29
Willow, 85
Windy, 29
Wiscus, 29
Wolsey, 85
Wolsey, Cardinal Thomas 85
Wong Mau, 72
World War I, 21, 37, 84
World War II, 21

Yankee, 72
Yeats, William Butler, 15
Yildiz, 64
Yildizcek, 64
Yo Yo, 85
Yul, 69

Zebra, 60
Zebrina, 60
Zizi, 29
Zola, Emile, 12
Zombi, 43
Zula, 66
Zuleika, 29